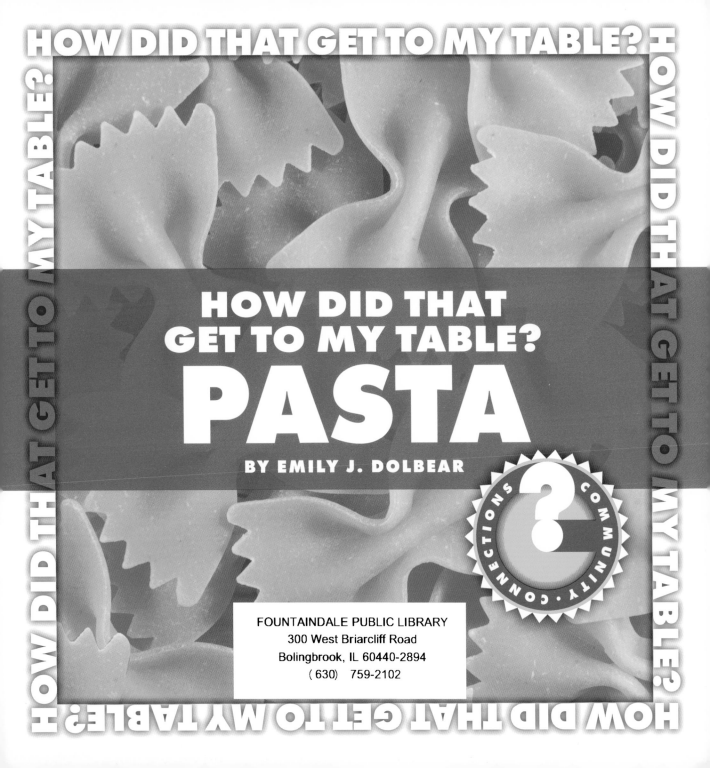

HOW DID THAT GET TO MY TABLE?
PASTA

BY EMILY J. DOLBEAR

Published in the United States of America by Cherry Lake Publishing
Ann Arbor, Michigan
www.cherrylakepublishing.com

Content Adviser: Anuradha Prakash, Professor of Food Science, Chapman University
Reading Adviser: Cecilia Minden-Cupp, PhD, Literacy Consultant

Photo Credits: Cover and page 1, ©iStockphoto.com/magnetcreative; page 5, ©iStockphoto.com/
Ju-Lee; page 7, ©iStockphoto.com/Grafissimo; page 9, ©iStockphoto.com/ImagineGolf; page 11,
©iStockphoto.com/imagestock; page 13, ©paolo negri/Alamy; page 15, ©iStockphoto.com/
redmal; page 17, ©iStockphoto.com/detchimo; page 19, ©iStockphoto.com/The-Tor; page 21,
©iStockphoto.com/realitybytes

LIBRARY OF CONGRESS CATALOGING-IN-PUBLICATION DATA
Dolbear, Emily J.
 How did that get to my table? Pasta / by Emily J. Dolbear.
   p. cm.—(Community connections)
 Includes index.
 ISBN-13: 978-1-60279-470-2
 ISBN-10: 1-60279-470-7
 1. Cookery (Pasta)—Juvenile literature. I. Title. II. Series.
 TX809.M17D66 2009
 664'.755—dc22   2008044185

Cherry Lake Publishing would like to acknowledge the
work of The Partnership for 21st Century Skills. Please
visit *www.21stcenturyskills.org* for more information.

CONTENTS

WHAT'S PASTA?

Are you ready for dinner? It's macaroni and cheese. Pasta might be one of your favorite foods. Do you ever wonder what pasta is made of or where it comes from? Let's find out how pasta gets to your dinner table.

Macaroni is just one kind of pasta.

FIELDS OF WHEAT

Most pasta comes from **wheat**. The wheat plants need sunshine and water to grow tall.

Farmers use a **combine** to collect the **grain** from the wheat plants. A combine cuts and separates the grains from the stalks.

A combine is a machine that helps make gathering wheat easier.

Do you know any farmers? Ask them some questions about farming. Do they grow wheat? What's hard about farming? What do they like about farming? Asking questions is a great way to learn.

What happens next? The grain is loaded into **grain elevators**. These large buildings keep the grain dry.

Trucks take the grain to a **mill**. Machines at the mill clean and grind the grain. This turns it into flour. The flour is packed into large bags. The bags are sent to pasta factories.

Grain elevators are large buildings for storing grain.

FROM FACTORY TO MARKET

Most pasta is made of wheat flour. How does the flour become the noodles in your soup?

At a factory, workers add water to the wheat flour to make **dough**. Sometimes eggs are added to the flour. This makes a golden pasta.

Pasta dough is soft and stretchy. Have you ever made dough at home?

THINK!

Sometimes vegetables are mixed into pasta dough. The vegetables make the dough different colors. Can you name a vegetable that would make green pasta? How about one that would make red pasta?

11

Pasta comes in many shapes and sizes. Machines at the factory press pasta dough through a special shaped hole. Or the machines roll and cut the pasta dough.

Then the pasta dries. Machines box or bag the dried pasta. Workers sometimes pack dried pasta by hand. They do that so the pasta doesn't break.

12

Machines turn the pasta dough into different shapes.

How does the factory pasta get to a store near you? It can travel in many ways. Ships, trains, and trucks help carry large boxes of pasta to stores. Workers at the store unpack the large boxes. Then they place the small packages of pasta on the shelves.

Big trucks carry pasta and other foods to stores.

15

You can find pasta in almost every food store. Large and small stores sell all kinds of pasta. What is your favorite type of pasta? What will you buy and take home to have for dinner?

Can you tell which of these pastas were made with vegetables?

LOOK!

Look at pasta packages on your kitchen shelves or at the market. Can you name five different shapes of pasta?

17

ON YOUR TABLE

Pasta is cooked by boiling the noodles in water. Pasta can take from 3 to 12 minutes to cook. Thicker noodles need more time to boil.

You can serve pasta with a sauce or filling. You can also eat pasta in soup. Can you think of other ways to serve pasta?

Pasta packages have cooking directions printed on them. The directions tell you how long to boil the noodles.

It's time to dig in to your macaroni and cheese. Now you know where it came from and how it was made. Why not tell your family how the pasta got to your dinner table?

The pasta in your bowl started out as wheat in a farmer's field.

MAKE A GUESS!

Can you guess what kind of pasta people like best? Ask five people to name their favorite kind of pasta. Did their answers match your guess? The National Pasta Association says that 40 percent of Americans like **spaghetti** best!

21

GLOSSARY

combine (KAHM-bine) a machine that cuts, cleans, and separates stalks from grain

dough (DOH) a thick mixture of flour, water, and other things that is used to make bread, pasta, or other foods

grain (GRAYN) the small, hard seeds of wheat, corn, or other cereal plants

grain elevators (GRAYN EL-uh-vay-turz) large buildings that store grain

macaroni (mak-uh-ROH-nee) dried, hollow tubes made of flour dough that are cooked by boiling

mill (MIL) a building with machines that grind grain into flour or meal

spaghetti (spuh-GET-ee) long strips of flour dough that are cooked by boiling

wheat (WEET) a grass that produces grain, often used to make flour

FIND OUT MORE

BOOKS

Bentley, Joyce. *Pasta*. North Mankato, MN: Chrysalis Education, 2006.

Martineau, Susan, and Hel James. *Bread, Rice, and Pasta*. North Mankato, MN: Smart Apple Media, 2007.

Mayo, Gretchen Will. *Pasta*. Milwaukee: Weekly Reader Early Learning Library, 2004.

WEB SITES

National Pasta Association—Pasta Shapes
www.ilovepasta.org/shapes.html
Learn to identify many different shapes of pasta

Wheat Foods Council—Amazing Wheat
www.wheatfoods.org/FlashForKids/index.html
Take a quiz, locate more resources, and get recipes

INDEX

ABOUT THE AUTHOR

Emily J. Dolbear works as a freelance editor and writer of children's books. She lives with her pasta-loving family in Brookline, Massachusetts.